I0105920

We Still Do:

10 WAYS TO LOVE MY HUSBAND

DR. LATINA C. CAMPBELL

Copyright © 2024 Latina C. Campbell

All rights reserved. No part of this book may be reproduced in any form or by any electronic or mechanical means, including information storage and retrieval systems, without permission in writing from the publisher, except by reviewers, who may quote brief passages in a review.

Print ISBN: 978-1-955312-91-2

eBook ISBN: 978-1-955312-92-9

Printed in the United States of America

Story Corner Publishing & Consulting, Inc.

Chesapeake, VA 23325

Storycornerpublishing@yahoo.com

www.StoryCornerPublishing.com

Dedication

I dedicate this book to every woman who does their best and long for the same in return. I hear you and have included you in my prayers. Also, please note LOVE is not a feeling, it is an action. Therefore, show love everyday even if it hurts.

"Love is patient, love is kind. It does not envy, it does not boast, it is not proud. It does not dishonor others, it is not self-seeking, it is not easily angered, it keeps no record of wrongs. Love does not delight in evil but rejoices with the truth. It always protects, always trusts, always hopes, always perseveres. Love never fails..." 1 Corinthians 13:4-8 NIV

Contents

Introduction 1
A LOVE WORTH CULTIVATING

Chapter 1 7
COMMUNICATE OPENLY

Chapter 2 13
SHOW APPRECIATION DAILY

Chapter 3 19
SEXUAL INTIMACY

Chapter 4 25
SUPPORT HIS DREAMS

Chapter 5 31
HONOR, RESPECT, AND SUBMISSION

Chapter 6 36
HANDLE CONFLICT WITH CARE

Chapter 7 41
FORGIVENESS, PATIENCE, AND AFFIRMATIONS

Chapter 8 47
MAINTAIN A SENSE OF HUMOR

Chapter 9 .... **53**
   BUILD A STRONG FRIENDSHIP

Chapter 10 .... **59**
   GROW TOGETHER SPIRITUALLY WITH GOD

Bonus Chapter... **65**
   HEALING THROUGH LOVE AND KINDNESS

Conclusion **71**
   GROWING IN LOVE DAILY

INTRODUCTION
A LOVE WORTH CULTIVATING

On December 22, 2016, my husband and I got married, and I was in awe of God because it was the fulfillment of a prayer I had since I was a young girl. Ironically, I met him in church after God led me there, and within a month, we were married. I had dotted all the I's and crossed all the T's. We did things God's way—no sex, no spending the night, just quality time together enjoying each other's company. When God told me he was the one and revealed that my husband-to-be was the gift He had prepared for me, I just knew everything would be *perfect*. Boy, was I wrong.

Let me clarify: my husband wasn't and isn't a bad man. But if it had been up to me, I would have left him within the first three months of our marriage! I hated everything about becoming "one" with him—it was overwhelming and exhausting. You see, no one told me that the process of two becoming one is *hard* work. If I hadn't had God guiding and coaching me every step of the way, I probably would've lost my mind—or worse. I didn't know what to expect, but it certainly wasn't what I experienced.

I tried my best to be what I thought was the "good wife." I cooked, cleaned, catered to him, showered him with gifts, kept things exciting, gave him quality time, listened to his needs, encouraged him, and even gave him the child he pressured me for, although I preferred to wait a while. But none of it brought me what I longed for—true love and the feeling of being seen and valued.

I don't think my husband intentionally took me for granted, but when someone is used to being catered to, they stop seeing it as special and start seeing it as expected. My husband, as the tall, good-looking, anointed preacher who could open Heaven with his singing, was constantly showered with attention. So, you can imagine the challenge I faced trying to stand out as more than just another person catering to him.

Despite the struggles, I was still honored when God told me that He sent this man to be my husband. I wanted to be the wife he needed, but over time, I began to feel overlooked and unappreciated. I became unfulfilled and ready to walk away. I prayed and fasted, crying out to God, "If You joined us together, why is this what our marriage looks like?" Eventually, we became little more than roommates, and I found myself holding on only for the sake of the kids. I was completely unhappy, burdened by traumatic experiences, and carrying the weight of our family on my own.

Every time I tried to take off my wedding rings, God would instruct me to put them back on—but He wouldn't answer my questions. I became angry with God over my husband and what our "marriage" had become. At one point, I didn't even consider myself married anymore. I just wanted peace and joy again, and I was convinced I wouldn't find them in a man. What I've learned now is that peace and joy only come from God. They will NEVER come from a man—and I mean *never*.

One day, I decided to stop wearing my emotions on my sleeve and asked God to show me my own faults—the things I was doing that brought out the worst in my husband. I firmly believe we have the power to bring out either the best or the worst in someone, and since I was only seeing the worst in my husband, I needed to know what I needed to change. Don't get me wrong, everyone—including my husband—has to be accountable for their own actions. But I had allowed bitterness and resentment to take root in my heart, and it made me wicked and far from love.

I wanted to do better, hoping it would inspire my husband to do the same since we are one. God reminded me of the love scriptures I had decorated our bedroom with when we got married and moved into our first home. He reminded me that love is an *action*, not a *feeling*. I used to tell God that I didn't *feel* loved by my husband, but God showed me that love is a requirement if we claim to be His children. Since God is love, if He is our Father, we are called to reflect Him in our lives— meaning we must also be love.

This revelation crushed me because my deepest desire is to please God, but I realized I was falling short every time I mirrored my husband's behavior instead of God's love. God also revealed to me that my husband didn't truly understand His love and didn't know how to be a husband. While God had prepared and trained me to be a wife before marriage, my husband hadn't been trained to be a husband, and he was too prideful to learn.

God wanted to use me to reach him, but I kept standing in the way with my emotions. God reminded me that my husband, above all else, belongs to Him and is my assignment. As wives, we are created to be helpmeets, which means coming alongside our husbands to help them fulfill the work God has called them to do. A husband may act as though he has it all together, but without his wife, he is incomplete.

That said, it's important to set healthy boundaries. Some husbands may take advantage of their wives' help, and it's okay to say "no." I had to learn this the hard way after depleting myself time and time again. God revealed that I was doing both my job and my husband's job, and that was not His will. Marriage and family responsibilities should be shared.

When I resubmitted my heart, mind, and soul back to God, everything changed. I stopped making my husband the center of my life—good or bad—and put God back in His rightful place as number one. I had been so consumed by the stress of my marriage that I pushed God aside, but I learned that God wants to lead us every step of the way. When we stray from Him, we leave ourselves vulnerable to attack.

Once I surrendered to God, He began to work within me, and that transformation sparked a change in my husband. He started seeing the damage his actions had caused, cut off negative influences, stepped into his role as a husband and father, and prioritized his family. Of course, this did not happen overnight. It was a process, but I hung in there trusting God.

This year, we will celebrate eight years of marriage, and we look forward to all things new. We continue to trust God to guide us on this journey, and we confidently say, "We still do."

Marriage is the first relationship God created, and He honors it. It is also one of the most profound relationships we can experience when we think of two people becoming one flesh. Marriage is a sacred bond or covenant that should be built on love, trust, respect, and mutual commitment. Yet, as much as love is often described as an effortless feeling, the truth is that sustaining and deepening that love requires effort, intentionality, and an ongoing commitment to growth.

This book, *We Still Do*, is not just about grand gestures or fleeting moments of romance; it is about cultivating a love that lasts through every season of life. It's about building a relationship where both partners feel seen, valued, and cherished, and where challenges become opportunities to grow closer rather than drift apart. Keep hope alive because it won't always be like this if you are in a dark part of marriage.

Why This Book Matters

Modern life is full of distractions and demands that can pull couples apart—work, parenting, personal goals, and even social media. In this fast-paced world, love can sometimes take a backseat, not because we care less but because we assume love will take care of itself. However, thriving marriages are not the result of chance but of choice. Choosing to prioritize your relationship, to communicate openly, to support each other, and to continuously invest in your partnership is what creates a bond that withstands the test of time.

This book provides practical, heartfelt strategies to help you not only love your husband better but also nurture the health and happiness of your marriage. Each chapter offers insights and actionable steps to make your love stronger, deeper, and more fulfilling. Whether you are newlyweds or have been together for decades, the principles here can help you rediscover and reimagine your love.

The Power of Intentional Love

Intentional love means choosing to love your partner in ways that speak to their heart, honor their individuality, and strengthen your connection. It is about creating a safe space for your partner to be themselves while also challenging each other to grow. Intentional love is not about perfection but persistence—it's about showing up for each other daily, even when it's hard.

This book explores topics that matter deeply in a marriage: communication, affection, trust, conflict resolution, and spiritual connection. It also touches on finding joy in the mundane, building a strong friendship, and embracing change as you grow together. These practices not only deepen your bond but also allow you to enjoy a more meaningful, satisfying relationship.

A Personal Invitation

As you read this book, I invite you to reflect on your own marriage. What are the strengths you bring to your relationship? Where are there opportunities for growth? More importantly, how can you love your husband in a way that makes him feel deeply cherished, respected, and valued?

This journey is not about losing yourself or neglecting your own needs. It's about balancing your individuality with a shared commitment to creating a life of love and partnership. By focusing on these principles, you can strengthen your marriage and create a foundation for joy, connection, and resilience.

Together, let's explore how you can show up for your husband, build a partnership that thrives, and cultivate a love that is truly worth celebrating. This is your guide to loving with purpose and passion—because your marriage deserves nothing less.

Welcome to the journey!

CHAPTER 1
COMMUNICATE OPENLY

The Heart of Connection

Open communication is the cornerstone of a healthy and thriving marriage. It is the bridge that connects two individuals, allowing them to share their thoughts, feelings, dreams, and concerns. Without it, misunderstandings and emotional distance can easily creep in. Communicating openly with your husband is not just about speaking—it's about creating an atmosphere where both partners feel safe to be vulnerable, understood, and valued.

Why Open Communication Matters

In marriage, communication is how you nurture understanding, resolve conflict, and build intimacy. When you communicate openly, you strengthen trust and create a foundation where both of you can grow together. It's not just about solving problems or exchanging information; it's about fostering a connection that deepens your bond.

Key Benefits of Open Communication in Marriage:

- Enhances emotional intimacy and understanding.

- Prevents misunderstandings and resentment.

- Builds trust and strengthens the partnership.

- Encourages collaboration in decision-making.

- Provides a safe space to share thoughts and feelings.

Practical Ways to Foster Open Communication

1. Listen to Understand, Not Just Respond

Effective communication starts with listening. Truly listening to your husband means focusing on his words, tone, and emotions without interrupting or preparing your rebuttal.

- **Show Active Listening:** Maintain eye contact, nod, and use affirming words like, "I hear you," or "Tell me more."

- **Ask Clarifying Questions:** If something is unclear, gently ask for clarification. For example, "What do you mean by that?" or "Can you explain how you're feeling?"

- **Resist the Urge to Fix:** Sometimes, your husband may not be looking for solutions but simply needs to be heard. Validate his feelings without immediately offering advice unless he asks for it.

2. Be Honest and Transparent

Honesty is essential for trust. Share your feelings, thoughts, and needs openly, even when they're difficult to express.

- **Use "I" Statements:** Frame your thoughts with "I feel" or "I think" rather than accusatory statements like "You always..." This approach reduces defensiveness and keeps the conversation constructive.

- **Avoid Bottling Things Up:** If something is bothering you, address it calmly rather than letting it fester. Suppressed feelings can lead to resentment over time.

- **Be Vulnerable:** Share your fears, insecurities, and dreams with your husband. Vulnerability invites intimacy and shows him that you trust him with your deepest self.

3. Create Regular Opportunities for Dialogue

In the hustle of daily life, meaningful conversations can often take a backseat. Make intentional efforts to create time for open dialogue.

- **Schedule "Talk Time":** Set aside uninterrupted time to connect without distractions like phones or TV.

- **Engage in Daily Check-Ins:** Ask each other questions like, "How was your day?" or "What's on your mind?" These simple exchanges keep you emotionally connected.

- **Use Date Nights for Deeper Conversations:** Go beyond surface-level topics during date nights. Discuss your dreams, goals, and reflections on your relationship.

4. Address Conflict Constructively

Conflict is inevitable, but how you handle it determines its impact on your marriage. Open communication during disagreements fosters resolution and growth.

- **Stay Calm and Respectful:** Avoid raising your voice or resorting to insults. A calm tone encourages productive dialogue.

- **Stick to the Issue at Hand:** Don't bring up past grievances or unrelated matters. Focus on resolving the current issue.

- **Seek to Understand, Not Win:** Instead of trying to "win" the argument, aim to understand your husband's perspective and find common ground.

5. Pay Attention to Nonverbal Communication

Communication isn't just about words; body language, facial expressions, and tone of voice convey powerful messages.

- **Be Mindful of Your Tone:** Speak with kindness and respect, even during disagreements.

- **Use Positive Body Language:** Lean in, face your husband, and avoid crossing your arms or looking away, which can signal disinterest or defensiveness.

- **Observe His Cues:** If your husband seems withdrawn or upset, gently ask if he wants to talk. Nonverbal cues often reveal what words cannot.

Overcoming Barriers to Open Communication

1. Fear of Judgment or Rejection

It's natural to fear being judged or misunderstood, especially when discussing sensitive topics. Reassure your husband that his thoughts and feelings are safe with you. Create a judgment-free zone where both of you can express yourselves freely.

2. Busy Schedules

Life's demands can make it difficult to prioritize communication. Be intentional about carving out time to connect, even if it's just a few minutes each day.

3. Past Misunderstandings

If past attempts at communication have led to conflict, it's easy to avoid certain topics. Commit to approaching sensitive subjects with patience, compassion, and a fresh perspective.

Deepening Intimacy Through Communication

Open communication is not just about problem-solving; it's also about building a deeper emotional connection. Share your dreams, reminisce about happy memories, and discuss your future together. These conversations bring you closer and remind you of the love and partnership you share.

Questions to Spark Connection:

- What's one thing you're excited about right now?
- What's a dream you've never shared with me before?
- How can I support you better?

A Love That Grows Through Words

Communicating openly is an ongoing process, not a one-time achievement. By listening with empathy, expressing yourself honestly, and creating space for meaningful dialogue, you nurture a love that grows deeper with time. Remember, communication is not just about talking—it's about understanding, connecting, and fostering a partnership that thrives on mutual respect and care.

Your journey to love begins with your words. Let them build bridges, strengthen trust, and create a marriage where both partners feel truly heard and cherished.

CHAPTER 2
SHOW APPRECIATION DAILY

The Power of Appreciation in Marriage

Appreciation is the lifeblood of a thriving relationship. It reminds your husband that he is valued, seen, and cherished. In the routine of daily life, it's easy to take each other's efforts and presence for granted. However, expressing appreciation regularly ensures that your husband feels acknowledged for who he is and what he does. This daily habit not only strengthens your bond but also creates an atmosphere of positivity and gratitude in your marriage.

Why Appreciation Matters

Appreciation fosters emotional connection and reaffirms the love and respect you have for each other. When your husband feels appreciated, he is more likely to reciprocate those feelings, creating a positive cycle of mutual respect and admiration. Neglecting appreciation, on the other hand, can lead to feelings of neglect or resentment, even if the love is still there.

Key Benefits of Showing Appreciation Daily:

- Boosts your husband's self-esteem and confidence.

- Reduces feelings of being taken for granted.

- Strengthens emotional intimacy and connection.

- Encourages a positive and supportive dynamic in the marriage.

- Reinforces the value of your partnership.

Practical Ways to Show Appreciation

1. Use Words to Express Gratitude

The simplest way to show appreciation is through verbal acknowledgment. Your words have the power to uplift and encourage your husband.

- **Say "Thank You" Often:** Don't assume he knows you appreciate him. Thank him for the little things, like taking out the trash, fixing something around the house, or simply being there for you.

- **Be Specific:** Instead of a generic "thanks," say, "Thank you for making time to help with the kids today; it really means a lot to me." Specificity shows that you notice and value his efforts.

- **Compliment Him:** Regularly highlight his strengths and qualities, such as his kindness, work ethic, or sense of humor. For example, "I love how you always find a way to make me laugh, even on hard days."

2. Show Appreciation Through Actions

Actions often speak louder than words. Small, thoughtful gestures can convey your appreciation in powerful ways.

- **Cook His Favorite Meal:** Surprise him with his favorite dish or dessert to show that you were thinking about him.

- **Leave Notes or Texts:** Write a heartfelt note or send a text during the day expressing your love and gratitude. A simple "I appreciate everything you do for our family" can make his day.

- **Help Him Out:** Offer to assist with something he usually handles, like running an errand or taking care of a task he dislikes.

3. Acknowledge His Efforts Publicly

Appreciating your husband in front of others can be especially meaningful. It shows him that you are proud of him and value his contributions.

- **Compliment Him in Front of Friends or Family:** Mention something you admire about him during gatherings, such as, "I'm so grateful for how supportive he's been with my goals lately."

- **Celebrate His Achievements:** Whether it's a work milestone or a personal victory, make a big deal out of his accomplishments. Plan a small celebration or toast to recognize his hard work.

4. Pay Attention to His Love Language

Understanding your husband's love language helps you show appreciation in ways that resonate most with him.

- **Words of Affirmation:** If he values verbal acknowledgment, focus on expressing your gratitude and admiration with kind words.

- **Acts of Service:** If he feels loved through actions, do something thoughtful, like taking care of a chore he dislikes.

- **Gifts:** If he enjoys receiving gifts, surprise him with something meaningful, like a book he's been wanting or a small token of your love.

- **Quality Time:** If he values time together, plan an activity or outing that he enjoys.

- **Physical Touch:** If touch is his love language, express appreciation through a hug, a kiss, or a back rub.

The Role of Consistency

While grand gestures are wonderful, it's the small, consistent acts of appreciation that have the most lasting impact. Daily expressions of gratitude become the foundation of a loving and affirming relationship.

Ways to Incorporate Daily Appreciation:

- Start each day by telling your husband one thing you're thankful for about him.

- End the day with a compliment or acknowledgment of something he did that day.

- Keep a gratitude journal where you jot down things you appreciate about him and share it with him periodically.

Overcoming Common Challenges

1. Feeling Too Busy to Show Appreciation

In the busyness of life, it can be easy to let appreciation slip through the cracks. However, expressing gratitude doesn't have to take much time. A quick note, a kind word, or a smile of acknowledgment can go a long way.

2. Taking His Efforts for Granted

It's natural to get used to the things your husband does regularly, such as going to work, helping with the kids, or fixing things around the house. Make an effort to notice these everyday contributions and express your gratitude.

3. Misunderstanding His Needs

Sometimes, the way you express appreciation may not fully resonate with your husband. Talk openly about what makes him feel appreciated and adjust your efforts accordingly.

The Ripple Effect of Gratitude

When you show appreciation daily, you set a positive tone for your marriage. Gratitude fosters a sense of partnership and reminds your husband that his efforts, presence, and love are valued. This habit can also inspire him to reciprocate, creating a marriage that thrives on mutual respect and affirmation.

Reflection Questions:

- What are three things I deeply appreciate about my husband?

- How can I express my gratitude to him in a meaningful way today?

- How can I be more consistent in noticing and acknowledging his efforts?

Showing appreciation daily is one of the most powerful ways to nurture your marriage. It strengthens your bond, deepens intimacy, and reminds both of you why you chose each other. When your husband feels valued and appreciated, he is more likely to flourish in the relationship, creating a positive cycle of love and gratitude that benefits you both.

Let your words and actions be a daily reminder of how much you value and cherish him. After all, appreciation is not just a feeling—it's a choice that breathes life into your marriage every single day.

CHAPTER 3
SEXUAL INTIMACY

A healthy sexual relationship is a vital part of a strong and thriving marriage. It is not only a physical act but also an emotional and spiritual connection that deepens the intimacy between you and your husband. When approached with love, care, and intentionality, fulfilling your husband's sexual desires can strengthen your bond and bring you closer as partners. This chapter will explore how to create a fulfilling sexual relationship, rooted in mutual respect, open communication, and a shared commitment to meeting each other's needs.

The Importance of Sexual Intimacy in Marriage

Sexual intimacy is a unique and sacred connection that sets marriage apart from all other relationships. It allows both partners to feel loved, desired, and valued. For many men, physical intimacy is a primary way they express and receive love, making it an essential part of the marital relationship.

1. A Physical Expression of Love:

Sex is a powerful way to express love, care, and devotion to your husband. It communicates affection and strengthens the emotional bond you share.

2. Boosting Emotional Connection:

A fulfilling sexual relationship can lead to greater emotional intimacy. When both partners feel satisfied and connected in this area, it often translates into better communication, trust, and overall harmony in the marriage.

3. Honoring God's Design for Marriage:

Sex within marriage is part of God's beautiful design. Embracing this gift allows you to glorify Him by nurturing your relationship in a way that aligns with His purpose for intimacy.

The Biblical Foundation of Sexual Intimacy

Sexual intimacy within marriage is a beautiful and sacred gift from God. Scripture highlights its importance in fostering unity and mutual satisfaction between husband and wife.

1. Sex as a Gift from God

"Let your fountain be blessed, and rejoice in the wife of your youth, a lovely deer, a graceful doe. Let her breasts fill you at all times with delight; be intoxicated always in her love." (Proverbs 5:18-19)

This verse celebrates the joy and satisfaction found in marital intimacy, emphasizing its role in delighting and strengthening your bond.

2. Mutual Fulfillment

"The husband should fulfill his marital duty to his wife, and likewise the wife to her husband. The wife does not have authority over her own body but yields it to her husband. In the same way, the husband does not have authority over his own body but yields it to his wife." (1 Corinthians 7:3-4)

This scripture highlights the mutual responsibility to meet each other's needs, fostering a partnership based on love and respect.

3. Unity in Marriage

"Therefore a man shall leave his father and mother and hold fast to his wife, and the two shall become one flesh." (Genesis 2:24)

Sexual intimacy is a reflection of the unity and oneness God intended for marriage. It deepens the emotional and spiritual connection between husband and wife.

Understanding Your Husband's Needs

Every individual is different, and understanding your husband's unique needs and desires is key to building a satisfying sexual relationship. This requires open communication, curiosity, and a willingness to prioritize each other's needs.

1. Talk About It:

Openly discuss your sexual relationship with your husband. Ask about his desires, preferences, and feelings, and share your own. This not only eliminates misunderstandings but also fosters deeper trust and intimacy.

2. Recognize the Emotional Aspect of Physical Intimacy:

While sex may seem primarily physical, it often carries significant emotional weight. When you make an effort to meet his desires, it communicates love, respect, and appreciation for him as a partner.

3. Learn His Love Language:

If physical touch is one of your husband's primary love languages, fulfilling his sexual desires may be especially important to him. Pay attention to how he expresses affection and consider how sex contributes to his feeling of being loved and valued.

Practical Ways to Fulfill Your Husband's Sexual Desires

1. Prioritize Intimacy:

Amid the busyness of daily life, it's easy to let intimacy take a backseat. Make a conscious effort to prioritize physical closeness, scheduling time for each other if necessary. Intimacy doesn't have to be spontaneous to be meaningful.

2. Be Present and Engaged:

When you are intimate with your husband, be fully present and engaged. Show enthusiasm and make an effort to connect emotionally as well as physically. Your willingness and effort mean as much as the act itself.

3. Keep the Spark Alive:

Routine can sometimes dull the excitement of a sexual relationship. Keep things fresh by trying new experiences together, whether it's changing up the setting, surprising him with romantic gestures, or exploring ways to deepen your connection.

4. Take Care of Yourself:

Your own confidence and comfort in your body can significantly affect your sexual relationship. Invest in self-care, wear something that makes you feel attractive, and communicate openly about what makes you feel comfortable and confident.

5. Respond to His Initiatives:

Your husband may express his sexual desires in subtle ways, such as through physical affection, compliments, or acts of service. Pay attention to these cues and respond with love and enthusiasm.

6. Create an Atmosphere for Intimacy:

Set the stage for intimacy by creating a warm, inviting environment. This might mean setting aside distractions, lighting candles, playing soft music, or simply ensuring you have time to connect without interruptions.

Balancing Sexual Intimacy and Your Needs

While fulfilling your husband's sexual desires is important, it's equally vital to ensure your own needs are being met. A healthy sexual relationship is built on mutual satisfaction, respect, and open communication.

1. Communicate Your Needs:

Be honest about your own desires, boundaries, and expectations. Your husband will likely appreciate your openness and be eager to meet your needs as well.

2. Establish a Safe Space:

Ensure that your sexual relationship is a safe space where both partners feel comfortable and respected. This includes being sensitive to each other's feelings, preferences, and comfort levels.

3. Embrace the Joy of Giving and Receiving:

True intimacy is about giving and receiving love selflessly. By focusing on each other's pleasure and connection, you create a relationship that is fulfilling for both of you.

The Spiritual Aspect of Sexual Intimacy

Sexual intimacy is not just physical or emotional—it is also deeply spiritual. It reflects the unity and oneness that God intended for marriage.

1. Pray for Your Intimacy:

Pray for your sexual relationship, asking God to help you grow closer and to bless this aspect of your marriage.

2. Unity Reflects God's Design

"So they are no longer two, but one flesh. Therefore what God has joined together, let no one separate." (Matthew 19:6)

Intimacy fosters unity and reminds you of the sacred bond you share as husband and wife.

3. Overcome Barriers with Grace:

If challenges arise in your sexual relationship, approach them with patience, grace, and a willingness to work together. Seek guidance from God, and if needed, consult a trusted counselor or mentor. "Be completely humble and gentle; be patient, bearing with one another in love." (Ephesians 4:2)

4. Honor Each Other:

A healthy sexual relationship requires mutual respect and a commitment to honoring each other as God's creation. By viewing intimacy as a way to glorify God, you can approach it with a deeper sense of purpose and love.

5. A Reflection of God's Love

"Above all, clothe yourselves with love, which binds everything together in perfect harmony." (Colossians 3:14)

Physical intimacy is one way to reflect God's love for your spouse, deepening your connection and glorifying Him through your marriage.

Reflection Questions

- How can you make your sexual relationship a greater priority in your marriage?

- What steps can you take to better understand and meet your husband's desires?

- How can you and your husband grow closer emotionally, spiritually, and physically through intimacy?

Fulfilling your husband's sexual desires is an act of love, care, and devotion that strengthens the bond between you. When approached with intentionality and mutual respect, sexual intimacy becomes more than a physical act—it becomes a reflection of your love for each other and for God. By prioritizing this sacred connection, you create a marriage that is not only satisfying but deeply fulfilling in every sense of the word. Let your love and commitment to each other shine through in all aspects of your relationship, including your intimate connection, as you continue to grow together in love and unity.

CHAPTER 4
SUPPORT HIS DREAMS

The Power of Believing in Him

Every person has dreams—goals and aspirations that give their life meaning and purpose. For your husband, these dreams may range from career ambitions to personal growth or creative passions. As his partner, your support plays a crucial role in helping him pursue those dreams. When you believe in your husband and actively support his aspirations, you not only nurture his confidence but also strengthen your marriage by fostering a partnership rooted in mutual respect and encouragement.

Why Supporting His Dreams Matters

Supporting your husband's dreams is a powerful way to show love and respect. It communicates that you value his passions and are invested in his success and happiness. Even if his dreams differ from your own or seem challenging, your encouragement can provide the motivation and confidence he needs to persevere.

Key Benefits of Supporting His Dreams:

- Builds trust and deepens emotional intimacy.

- Strengthens his self-confidence and sense of purpose.

- Demonstrates that you're a team, working toward shared and individual goals.

- Inspires him to reciprocate and support your dreams.

- Enhances communication and mutual understanding.

Practical Ways to Support His Dreams

1. Listen to His Goals and Aspirations

Understanding your husband's dreams starts with active listening. Create space for him to share his hopes, ambitions, and concerns.

- **Ask Open-Ended Questions:** Encourage him to talk about his dreams by asking questions like, "What excites you most about this goal?" or "How can I support you in this journey?"

- **Listen Without Judgment:** Avoid dismissing his ideas, even if they seem ambitious or out of the box. Instead, express curiosity and genuine interest.

- **Validate His Feelings:** Acknowledge his passion and dedication by saying things like, "I love how much this means to you" or "I admire your determination."

2. Be His Biggest Cheerleader

Your belief in your husband can be a source of strength and encouragement as he works toward his goals.

- **Offer Words of Encouragement:** Remind him of his strengths and capabilities. For example, "I know you can do this because you're so talented and hardworking."

- **Celebrate His Wins:** Whether big or small, acknowledge his achievements and milestones with genuine enthusiasm.

- **Stay Positive During Challenges:** When setbacks occur, help him stay motivated by focusing on solutions and reminding him of his progress.

3. Share in the Journey

Being an active participant in your husband's journey shows that you're invested in his success.

- **Collaborate on Planning:** Offer to help him map out steps to achieve his goals, such as creating a timeline or brainstorming strategies.

- **Offer Practical Support:** Help in tangible ways, like managing household responsibilities to free up his time or connecting him with resources and opportunities.

- **Learn About His Passion:** Take an interest in what he's pursuing by reading about it, attending related events, or asking thoughtful questions.

4. Balance Support with Honest Feedback

While unconditional support is important, being honest when needed can help your husband approach his goals with clarity and realism.

- **Encourage Realistic Planning:** If his goals require significant time, money, or effort, discuss how to achieve them in a way that aligns with your shared priorities.
- **Frame Feedback Positively:** When offering constructive feedback, focus on solutions and express your belief in his ability to overcome challenges.
- **Avoid Criticism:** Instead of pointing out flaws or weaknesses, emphasize growth and the potential for improvement.

5. Support Him Emotionally

Pursuing dreams can be emotionally taxing, especially when facing obstacles or self-doubt. Be his source of comfort and reassurance.

- **Offer a Listening Ear:** Let him vent or share his frustrations without feeling the need to solve everything.

- **Remind Him of His Worth:** Reinforce that his value isn't tied solely to his success but also to who he is as a person.

- **Encourage Self-Care:** Remind him to take breaks and prioritize his well-being as he works toward his goals.

Overcoming Challenges in Supporting His Dreams

1. Balancing His Dreams with Family Responsibilities

Sometimes, pursuing big dreams can require sacrifices, like time or financial resources. Work together to find a balance that supports his aspirations while maintaining stability for your family.

- **Communicate Openly:** Discuss how his goals impact both of you and collaborate on ways to manage responsibilities.

- **Share the Load:** Divide tasks or adjust schedules to ensure both partners feel supported.

2. Differences in Aspirations

You may not always fully understand or agree with his dreams, but you can still support them.

- **Respect His Individuality:** Recognize that his passions are part of what makes him unique.

- **Find Common Ground:** Look for ways his dreams can align with your shared values or goals.

3. Fear of Failure

Pursuing big dreams often comes with the risk of failure. Instead of focusing on potential outcomes, focus on the growth and fulfillment he gains from the journey.

- **Encourage Resilience:** Remind him that setbacks are part of the process and don't define his worth.

- **Celebrate Effort Over Results:** Highlight the courage and dedication he's shown, regardless of the outcome.

The Role of Mutual Support in Marriage

Supporting your husband's dreams fosters a partnership where both individuals feel valued and empowered. It also sets an example of mutual respect and encouragement that can inspire him to support your aspirations as well. Together, you create a relationship that uplifts and motivates both of you to reach your fullest potential.

Reflection Questions

- What are your husband's biggest dreams and goals?

- How can you actively support him in pursuing these aspirations?

- What challenges might arise, and how can you work through them together?

Supporting your husband's dreams is an act of love and partnership. It's about believing in his potential, encouraging his growth, and standing by him through the highs and lows. Your unwavering support not only helps him achieve his goals but also strengthens your bond as you navigate life's challenges together.

By cheering him on, sharing in his journey, and celebrating his efforts, you demonstrate that his happiness and fulfillment are as important to you as they are to him. In doing so, you build a marriage that thrives on shared dreams, mutual respect, and the joy of watching each other grow.

CHAPTER 5
HONOR, RESPECT, AND SUBMISSION

Marriage is a divine partnership designed by God, where both husband and wife are called to honor and serve one another. As a wife, showing honor, respect, and submitting to your husband reflects your obedience to God's Word and allows your marriage to flourish. Submission is often misunderstood in today's culture, but biblically, it is about mutual love, respect, and trust, rooted in God's purpose for marriage. This chapter will explore the beauty of honoring and submitting to your husband as an act of love and faithfulness to God, with guidance from Scripture.

Biblical Submission: What It Is and What It Is Not

Submission in marriage, as outlined in the Bible, is a voluntary act of love, respect, and trust that reflects the order God has established. It is not about inferiority, control, or dominance but about fulfilling the roles God has designed for both husband and wife.

1. Submission Is Rooted in God's Design

"Wives, submit to your own husbands as you do to the Lord. For the husband is the head of the wife as Christ is the head of the church, his body, of which he is the Savior." (Ephesians 5:22-23)

This verse highlights the divine order within marriage, where the husband is called to lead, and the wife is called to support him in a spirit of love and unity.

2. Submission Is Not Inferiority

"There is neither Jew nor Gentile, neither slave nor free, nor is there male and female, for you are all one in Christ Jesus." (Galatians 3:28)

While husbands and wives have distinct roles, both are equal in value and worth before God. Submission is not about diminishing a wife's identity but about embracing her role within the marriage.

3. Submission Requires Love and Mutual Respect

"Submit to one another out of reverence for Christ." (Ephesians 5:21)

Biblical submission is a two-way street. While wives are called to submit, husbands are called to love their wives sacrificially, mirroring Christ's love for the church.

The Role of Respect in Submission

Respecting your husband is a cornerstone of biblical submission. Respect is not only commanded by God but also deeply resonates with most men as a vital expression of love.

1. Respect as a Command

"However, let each one of you love his wife as himself, and let the wife see that she respects her husband." (Ephesians 5:33)

Respecting your husband means valuing his leadership, speaking to him with kindness, and honoring his role in your family.

2. Respect Through Words and Actions

"The wise woman builds her house, but with her own hands the foolish one tears hers down." (Proverbs 14:1)

Show respect by uplifting your husband through encouraging words, avoiding criticism, and supporting him in his decisions.

3. Respect in Public and Private

Honor your husband not only in private but also in how you speak about him to others. Publicly supporting your husband strengthens his confidence and your unity as a couple.

What Submission Looks Like in Practice

Submission is an active expression of trust in God and in your husband's leadership. It requires humility, grace, and a willingness to prioritize the good of your marriage over personal preferences.

1. Trusting His Leadership

"The heart of her husband trusts in her, and he will have no lack of gain." (Proverbs 31:11)

Trusting your husband's leadership means believing in his ability to make decisions for your family, even when you may not fully agree.

2. Supporting His Decisions

Submitting does not mean you don't have a voice. Instead, it means sharing your thoughts respectfully and allowing him to lead with the confidence that you are on his side.

3. Seeking Unity, Not Control

"Do nothing out of selfish ambition or vain conceit. Rather, in humility value others above yourselves." (Philippians 2:3)

Submission is about working together for the good of the marriage, not asserting control or demanding your way.

Honoring Your Husband

Honoring your husband means recognizing and celebrating his God-given role as the leader of your household. This act of honor reflects your reverence for God and your commitment to building a strong, godly marriage.

1. Speak Words of Affirmation

"Gracious words are a honeycomb, sweet to the soul and healing to the bones." (Proverbs 16:24)

Build up your husband with words that affirm his efforts, character, and leadership. Let him know you see and appreciate his contributions to your family.

2. Celebrate His Strengths

Focus on your husband's strengths rather than his weaknesses. Encourage him to pursue his goals and acknowledge his achievements, both big and small.

3. Serve with a Willing Heart

"She opens her hand to the poor and reaches out her hands to the needy." (Proverbs 31:20)

Serving your husband and family with joy and a willing spirit is a powerful way to show honor and respect.

The Spiritual Significance of Submission

Submission is ultimately an act of faith. By trusting your husband's leadership, you demonstrate your trust in God's plan for your marriage.

1. Submission as Worship

"And whatever you do, whether in word or deed, do it all in the name of the Lord Jesus, giving thanks to God the Father through him." (Colossians 3:17)

When you submit to your husband, you honor God by fulfilling your role within His divine design for marriage.

2. Reflecting Christ's Example

"Whoever wants to become great among you must be your servant, and whoever wants to be first must be your slave—just as the Son of Man did not come to be served, but to serve." (Matthew 20:26-28)

Christ modeled submission through His willingness to serve others. Following His example brings glory to God and strengthens your relationship with your husband.

3. A Testament to Others

"In the same way, let your light shine before others, that they may see your good deeds and glorify your Father in heaven." (Matthew 5:16)

Your loving submission and respect for your husband serve as a testimony to others about God's design for marriage.

Reflection Questions

- How can you show honor and respect to your husband in both words and actions?

- What steps can you take to better trust your husband's leadership?

- How can you embrace submission as an act of faith and obedience to God?

Honoring, respecting, and submitting to your husband is not about losing your voice or identity—it's about building a marriage that reflects God's love and design. By choosing to honor your husband, you fulfill your God-given role as a wife and strengthen the foundation of your relationship. Through trust, respect, and a spirit of humility, you create a partnership that glorifies God and serves as a shining example of His grace. As you walk in obedience to His Word, may your marriage be a testament to the beauty of love, unity, and mutual submission in Christ.

CHAPTER 6
HANDLE CONFLICT WITH CARE

The Reality of Conflict in Marriage

Every marriage encounters conflict. Disagreements and differences of opinion are inevitable when two people share their lives. However, the way you handle conflict can either strengthen your relationship or create distance. When approached with care, conflict becomes an opportunity for growth, understanding, and deepened intimacy.

This chapter focuses on strategies to handle conflict in ways that preserve respect, build trust, and ensure both partners feel heard and valued.

Why Handling Conflict with Care Matters

Conflict itself is not harmful—it's how you respond to it that determines its impact on your relationship. Poorly managed conflict can lead to resentment, frustration, and emotional distance. On the other hand, thoughtful conflict resolution fosters connection and ensures that both partners' needs are addressed.

Benefits of Handling Conflict with Care:

- Builds emotional safety and trust.

- Prevents issues from escalating into larger problems.

- Enhances communication and understanding.

- Encourages teamwork in resolving challenges.

- Strengthens the foundation of your relationship.

Principles of Healthy Conflict Resolution

1. Approach Conflict with a Team Mindset

Remember, it's not you versus your husband—it's both of you versus the problem. Viewing yourselves as a team shifts the focus from blame to collaboration.

- **Use "We" Statements:** Frame discussions around shared goals, such as, "How can we work through this together?"

- **Focus on Solutions:** Instead of dwelling on the problem, brainstorm ways to address it as a team.

2. Communicate with Respect

Respectful communication is key to resolving conflict effectively. Even in heated moments, choose words and tones that reflect love and care.

- **Avoid Insults and Blame:** Focus on the issue at hand, not personal attacks. Replace "You always..." with "I feel hurt when..."

- **Be Mindful of Your Tone:** A calm, measured tone helps prevent escalation and encourages productive dialogue.

3. Listen to Understand, Not Just to Respond

Listening is a cornerstone of conflict resolution. When your husband feels truly heard, he's more likely to engage in open and honest communication.

- **Practice Active Listening:** Repeat back what he says to ensure understanding, such as, "So you're saying that you felt overlooked when..."

- **Validate His Feelings:** Acknowledge his emotions, even if you disagree. For example, "I can see why you'd feel frustrated about that."

4. Take Responsibility for Your Part

Conflict often involves contributions from both partners. Acknowledging your role demonstrates maturity and a commitment to improving the relationship.

- **Admit Mistakes:** If you've made an error, apologize sincerely and specifically. For example, "I'm sorry I raised my voice earlier."

- **Avoid Defensiveness:** Instead of justifying your actions, focus on understanding your husband's perspective.

5. Manage Emotions Before Engaging

When emotions run high, it's easy to say or do things you regret. Taking time to cool off before discussing the issue can lead to more productive conversations.

- **Pause and Reflect:** If needed, step away briefly to collect your thoughts and emotions.

- **Use "I" Statements:** Express your feelings without assigning blame, such as, "I felt hurt when you didn't consult me about that decision."

Steps to Handle Conflict with Care

1. Set the Stage for a Constructive Conversation

Choose the right time and place to discuss sensitive topics.

- **Pick a Calm Environment:** Avoid addressing issues in the heat of the moment or in public settings.

- **Agree on Timing:** Ask, "Is this a good time to talk about something that's been on my mind?"

2. Focus on the Issue, Not the Person

Keep the discussion centered on the specific problem rather than generalizing or attacking character.

- **Be Specific:** Instead of saying, "You never listen to me," say, "I felt unheard when you didn't respond to my question earlier."

- **Avoid Bringing Up the Past:** Stick to the current issue rather than rehashing old conflicts.

3. Seek to Understand His Perspective

Conflict resolution requires empathy and a willingness to see things from your husband's point of view.

- **Ask Clarifying Questions:** For example, "Can you explain more about why that upset you?"

- **Acknowledge Valid Points:** Even if you disagree, find areas of agreement to build on.

4. Work Toward a Solution Together

After discussing the issue, collaborate on a resolution that feels fair and satisfying to both of you.

- **Brainstorm Options:** Ask, "What can we do differently next time to prevent this?"

- **Agree on Action Steps:** Ensure both partners are clear on what changes will be made.

5. Reconnect After the Conflict

Once the issue is resolved, take time to reaffirm your love and commitment to each other.

- **Express Gratitude:** Thank him for listening and working through the issue with you.

- **Show Affection:** A hug, kiss, or kind word can help repair any lingering tension.

Avoiding Common Pitfalls in Conflict

1. Stonewalling

Shutting down or withdrawing during conflict prevents resolution. Instead, communicate your need for space and agree to revisit the discussion later.

2. Escalation

Raising your voice or making inflammatory statements escalates the situation. Stay calm and focused on the issue.

3. Avoiding Conflict Altogether

Ignoring problems can lead to resentment. Address issues as they arise, even if they're uncomfortable to discuss.

Using Conflict to Strengthen Your Marriage

Conflict, when handled with care, can bring you closer to your husband. It provides opportunities to learn more about each other, deepen your understanding, and build trust. By approaching disagreements with love and respect, you create a relationship where both partners feel valued and heard.

Reflection Questions

- How do you typically respond to conflict in your marriage?

- Are there patterns or habits you could adjust to handle conflict more effectively?

- What steps can you take to create a safe and respectful environment for resolving disagreements?

Handling conflict with care is about prioritizing the health of your marriage over the desire to "win" an argument. It requires patience, empathy, and a commitment to working through challenges as a team.

By fostering open communication, active listening, and mutual respect, you transform conflict into a tool for growth and connection. Remember, the goal isn't to avoid disagreements altogether but to navigate them in a way that strengthens your bond and reaffirms your love for one another.

CHAPTER 7
FORGIVENESS, PATIENCE, AND AFFIRMATIONS

Marriage is a journey of two imperfect people striving to love each other deeply despite challenges and flaws. In this journey, forgiveness, patience, and affirmations play pivotal roles in nurturing a healthy and God-honoring relationship. These virtues are essential for overcoming conflicts, healing wounds, and building an environment of love and respect. As wives, choosing to extend grace, exhibit patience, and speak life through affirmations not only strengthens your bond with your husband but also pleases God.

The Power of Forgiveness

Forgiveness is at the heart of every thriving marriage. It allows you to release resentment, heal emotional wounds, and move forward in unity with your husband.

1. Forgiveness Reflects God's Grace

"Be kind and compassionate to one another, forgiving each other, just as in Christ God forgave you." (Ephesians 4:32)

Forgiveness in marriage mirrors the grace God extends to us daily. When you forgive your husband, you demonstrate Christ's love and mercy.

2. Forgiveness Releases Resentment

Holding onto grudges or past offenses can create emotional walls and strain your marriage. Forgiveness allows you to let go of bitterness and focus on building a stronger connection.

3. Forgiveness Is a Choice

Forgiveness is not always easy, but it is a decision you make out of love and commitment. By choosing to forgive, you prioritize your marriage over your hurt.

Practical Steps to Forgive:

- Pray for God's strength to forgive, especially in difficult moments.

- Communicate openly with your husband about how you feel.

- Focus on resolving issues instead of replaying past offenses.

Cultivating Patience in Marriage

Patience is the ability to endure challenges and shortcomings with grace and understanding. It is a vital virtue in marriage, especially when facing differences or disagreements.

1. Patience as an Act of Love

"Love is patient, love is kind. It does not envy, it does not boast, it is not proud." (1 Corinthians 13:4)

Patience is one of the key attributes of love. By showing patience toward your husband, you demonstrate your commitment to loving him unconditionally.

2. Patience Requires Humility

Being patient means acknowledging that both you and your husband are works in progress. It allows you to extend grace as he grows and learns, just as you would want him to do for you.

3. Patience Strengthens Your Bond

When you respond to challenges with patience instead of frustration, you create an atmosphere of peace and trust in your marriage.

Practical Ways to Show Patience:

- Take a moment to pause and pray before reacting to frustrating situations.

- Remember your husband's positive traits when his flaws test your patience.

- Focus on solutions rather than the problem at hand.

The Impact of Affirmations

Affirmations are powerful tools that build your husband's confidence, reinforce his worth, and strengthen your emotional connection. By affirming your husband, you create a marriage rooted in encouragement and mutual respect.

1. Words Have Power

"The tongue has the power of life and death, and those who love it will eat its fruit." (Proverbs 18:21)

Your words have the ability to uplift or tear down. Choosing to affirm your husband with kind and positive words strengthens his spirit and your relationship.

2. Affirmations Foster a Positive Environment

Speaking life into your husband helps create a marriage filled with gratitude and positivity. When your husband feels appreciated and valued, he is more likely to reciprocate with love and care.

3. Affirmations Build Confidence

Men often thrive on respect and affirmation. By acknowledging your husband's efforts, strengths, and contributions, you bolster his confidence and encourage him to continue growing.

Examples of Affirming Words:

- "I'm so proud of the way you provide for our family."

- "You are an amazing father and husband."

- "I appreciate all the little things you do for me."

- "I believe in you and your dreams."

The Connection Between Forgiveness, Patience, and Affirmations

Forgiveness, patience, and affirmations are interconnected. When you forgive your husband, you free yourself to be patient with his imperfections. When you are patient, you create the space to affirm his strengths and encourage his growth. Together, these virtues form the foundation of a loving, resilient, and God-centered marriage.

1. Forgiveness Brings Healing

Forgiveness removes barriers of hurt and resentment, paving the way for positive communication and affirmations.

2. Patience Creates Space for Growth

Patience allows your husband to grow and learn without fear of harsh criticism.

3. Affirmations Strengthen Emotional Bonds

Affirming your husband fosters emotional intimacy and reassures him of your love and support.

Spiritual Insights

Forgiveness Honors God

"For if you forgive other people when they sin against you, your heavenly Father will also forgive you." (Matthew 6:14)

Forgiving your husband is an act of obedience to God and reflects your faith in His plan for your marriage.

Patience Reflects God's Character

"The Lord is compassionate and gracious, slow to anger, abounding in love." (Psalm 103:8)

When you exhibit patience, you emulate God's loving and forgiving nature, bringing peace to your marriage.

Affirmations Reflect God's Encouragement

"Therefore encourage one another and build each other up, just as in fact you are doing." (1 Thessalonians 5:11)

Speaking affirmations aligns with God's desire for us to build each other up and strengthen our relationships.

Reflection Questions

- Are there any areas in your marriage where you need to extend forgiveness to your husband?

- How can you practice patience more intentionally in your daily interactions?

- What affirmations can you speak to your husband today to show him love and appreciation?

Forgiveness, patience, and affirmations are essential ingredients for a thriving marriage. By forgiving your husband, you release past hurts and focus on the future. Through patience, you create an atmosphere of love and understanding, allowing your relationship to grow. And with affirmations, you nurture his heart and strengthen your bond. These virtues not only transform your marriage but also glorify God, reflecting His grace, love, and encouragement in your relationship. Let forgiveness, patience, and affirmations be the daily expressions of your commitment to a Christ-centered marriage.

CHAPTER 8
MAINTAIN A SENSE OF HUMOR

The Healing Power of Laughter

Laughter is one of the simplest yet most powerful ways to strengthen a marriage. Life is full of unexpected challenges, and humor helps you navigate them with grace. By maintaining a sense of humor, you can diffuse tension, foster connection, and keep the joy alive in your relationship.

This chapter delves into why humor is essential in marriage, how it enhances emotional and relational health, and practical ways to incorporate it into your daily life.

Why Humor Matters in Marriage

Humor serves as a reminder that not every moment has to be serious, even when facing difficulties. It creates a light-hearted atmosphere that encourages emotional intimacy and trust.

Benefits of Maintaining a Sense of Humor:

- Helps diffuse conflict and reduce stress.

- Creates shared moments of joy and connection.

- Makes difficult situations feel more manageable.

- Builds a positive association with your partner.

- Encourages resilience in the face of life's challenges.

Couples who laugh together often report higher levels of satisfaction and connection in their marriages.

The Role of Humor in a Healthy Marriage

1. Humor as a Bonding Tool

Inside jokes, shared laughter, and playful teasing create a unique bond between you and your husband. These moments remind you of the joy you share and strengthen your connection.

- **Shared Memories:** Reflecting on funny moments from your past helps reinforce your shared history.

- **Playful Interactions:** A light-hearted attitude can transform mundane moments into opportunities for connection.

2. Humor as Stress Relief

When life feels overwhelming, humor provides a much-needed break from the seriousness of day-to-day responsibilities.

- **Lighten the Mood:** A well-timed joke or playful comment can defuse tension during stressful situations.

- **Shift Perspectives:** Laughter helps you see problems from a less intimidating angle, making them easier to tackle together.

3. Humor in Conflict Resolution

Used appropriately, humor can soften the edges of disagreements and remind you both not to take yourselves too seriously.

- **Break the Ice:** A funny comment or silly face during an argument can ease tension and pave the way for constructive dialogue.

- **Redirect Frustration:** Humor helps to refocus energy away from blame and toward collaboration.

How to Cultivate Humor in Your Marriage

1. Don't Take Yourself Too Seriously

Being able to laugh at yourself shows humility and encourages your husband to do the same.

- **Share Embarrassing Stories:** Open up about funny mistakes or awkward moments—it makes you more relatable.

- **Celebrate Imperfections:** Embrace the quirks and oddities that make you both unique.

2. Create Opportunities for Laughter

Make humor a regular part of your relationship by seeking out fun experiences together.

- **Watch Comedy Together:** Enjoy a funny movie, stand-up show, or sitcom as a way to unwind and connect.

- **Try Something New:** Activities like karaoke, board games, or escape rooms often lead to laughter and bonding.

3. Develop Inside Jokes

Inside jokes are a special way to connect on a deeper level.

- **Reflect on Shared Experiences:** Turn silly or memorable moments into recurring jokes.

- **Playfully Reference Quirks:** Lovingly tease each other about habits or preferences in a way that feels endearing.

4. Play Together

Playfulness keeps your relationship fresh and vibrant.

- **Engage in Playful Banter:** A little light teasing or a mock competition can bring out laughter and affection.

- **Be Spontaneous:** Surprise him with a silly dance, a funny meme, or a lighthearted prank.

5. Laugh Through Challenges

Even in tough times, humor can provide a sense of hope and resilience.

- **Find the Silver Lining:** Look for the absurdity or irony in challenging situations.

- **Lean on Each Other:** Laugh together about mishaps, whether it's burning dinner or getting caught in the rain.

The Dos and Don'ts of Humor in Marriage

Do:

- Use humor to build connection, not create distance.

- Be sensitive to your husband's mood and boundaries.

- Laugh with your partner, not at them.

- Use humor to celebrate, not criticize.

Don't:

- Use humor to mask deeper issues or avoid serious discussions.

- Make jokes at your partner's expense that might hurt their feelings.

- Rely on sarcasm or passive-aggressive humor, as it can breed resentment.

Real-Life Examples of Humor in Marriage

1. Turning an Argument into a Laugh

During a disagreement about how to assemble a piece of furniture, you might say, "Maybe we should call the manufacturer and tell them their instructions ruined our marriage!" This humorous exaggeration can lighten the mood and refocus both of you on teamwork.

2. Finding Humor in Mishaps

Imagine you both get lost on a road trip. Instead of getting frustrated, you might say, "Well, this is just our GPS's way of adding a little adventure to our day!" Such humor helps turn a stressful situation into a shared memory.

3. Sharing Silly Moments

When doing mundane chores, add a little fun by singing a parody of your favorite song or pretending to host a "cooking show" while making dinner together.

Reflection Questions

- When was the last time you and your husband shared a good laugh?

- How do you typically respond to challenges—can you find humor in them?

- What are some ways you can incorporate more playfulness into your daily interactions?

Laughter truly is the best medicine, not just for individuals but for marriages as well. By maintaining a sense of humor, you create an atmosphere of joy, resilience, and connection in your relationship.

Life may not always go as planned, but your ability to laugh together transforms everyday moments—both good and challenging—into opportunities for love and bonding. Keep finding reasons to smile, giggle, and belly laugh with your husband. After all, a marriage filled with laughter is a marriage filled with life.

CHAPTER 9
BUILD A STRONG FRIENDSHIP

The Foundation of a Lasting Marriage

A strong friendship is the cornerstone of a healthy and enduring marriage. While romance may ebb and flow over the years, friendship serves as a steady anchor, offering support, companionship, and understanding. When your spouse is also your best friend, you create a bond that weathers life's storms and deepens your connection over time.

This chapter explores the essential elements of a strong friendship in marriage, how to nurture it, and why it's the key to a thriving relationship.

Why Friendship Matters in Marriage

Romantic love is often celebrated in relationships, but friendship is the foundation that sustains a marriage over the long term.

- **Friendship Creates Stability:** It provides a sense of safety, trust, and reliability in the relationship.

- **Friendship Enhances Communication:** Friends talk openly, listen without judgment, and offer support.

- **Friendship Strengthens Emotional Intimacy:** It fosters a deeper understanding of each other's needs, desires, and dreams.

Couples who prioritize their friendship tend to have happier, more satisfying relationships because they genuinely enjoy each other's company.

Characteristics of a Strong Friendship in Marriage

1. Trust and Loyalty

A strong friendship is built on the assurance that your spouse has your back, no matter what.

- **Confidentiality:** Honor your partner's trust by keeping private conversations between the two of you.

- **Consistency:** Be dependable, showing your spouse they can rely on you.

2. Mutual Respect

Friends respect each other's individuality and value their differences.

- **Celebrate Each Other:** Recognize and appreciate your spouse's unique qualities.

- **Avoid Criticism:** Be mindful of how you speak to and about your partner.

3. Shared Interests and Activities

Friends enjoy spending time together and discovering common interests.

- **Find Hobbies You Both Love:** Explore activities like hiking, cooking, or playing games that you can enjoy together.

- **Create Rituals:** Establish traditions like Friday movie nights or morning coffee chats.

4. Support During Difficult Times

A true friend is there during the highs and lows of life.

- **Be Present:** Offer a listening ear and a shoulder to lean on when your spouse faces challenges.

- **Encourage Growth:** Support their personal and professional aspirations.

5. Genuine Enjoyment of Each Other's Company

Friendship thrives on laughter, shared moments, and a sense of fun.

- **Make Time for Fun:** Prioritize playfulness and light-hearted moments in your relationship.

- **Be Yourself:** Allow each other to relax and be authentic without fear of judgment.

How to Build and Strengthen Friendship in Marriage

1. Spend Quality Time Together

Friendship requires time and attention.

- **Schedule Regular "Friendship Dates":** Go beyond romantic dinners and spend time doing things you both enjoy as friends.

- **Engage in Deep Conversations:** Talk about your dreams, fears, and experiences to deepen your bond.

2. Show Interest in Each Other's Lives

Take an active interest in your husband's passions, hobbies, and goals.

- **Ask Questions:** Show curiosity about his day, interests, or new projects.

- **Participate When Possible:** Even if you don't share the same passion, your involvement shows support and care.

3. Prioritize Communication

Good friends talk openly and listen attentively.

- **Be Honest:** Share your thoughts and feelings honestly but kindly.

- **Practice Active Listening:** Give your spouse your full attention when they're speaking, and respond thoughtfully.

4. Share Laughter and Fun

Find ways to infuse joy into your marriage.

- **Recall Funny Memories:** Reflect on humorous or silly moments you've shared.

- **Try New Adventures:** Do something spontaneous or out of the ordinary to create new fun memories.

5. Be Each Other's Cheerleader

Encourage and uplift your husband, just as a friend would.

- **Celebrate Victories:** Whether big or small, acknowledge and celebrate his accomplishments.

- **Offer Encouragement:** When he's feeling down or doubtful, remind him of his strengths and potential.

6. Be Patient and Forgiving

Friendship thrives on grace and understanding.

- **Give the Benefit of the Doubt:** Assume good intentions when misunderstandings arise.

- **Let Go of Grudges:** Choose forgiveness over holding onto resentment.

7. Create Shared Goals

Friends often bond over a shared vision or purpose.

- **Plan for the Future Together:** Discuss your hopes and dreams as a couple.

- **Work Toward Common Goals:** Collaborate on projects like saving for a trip, redecorating your home, or starting a business.

Friendship in Everyday Moments

1. Celebrate the Small Things

Friends find joy in the little moments. Whether it's sharing a cup of coffee in the morning or laughing over an inside joke, these small interactions build connection.

2. Be Playful

Keep the friendship alive by embracing playfulness. A pillow fight, a funny text message, or a surprise gift can go a long way.

3. Support Each Other's Individuality

True friendship respects individuality. Encourage your husband to pursue his interests, even if they're different from your own.

4. Have Each Other's Back

Whether it's standing up for him in a social situation or helping him through a rough patch, being his ally reinforces your bond.

Challenges to Building Friendship in Marriage

1. Busy Schedules

Time constraints can make it difficult to connect as friends.

- **Solution**: Schedule time for each other, even if it's just 15 minutes a day to catch up.

2. Taking Each Other for Granted

Over time, it's easy to overlook the importance of nurturing your friendship.

- **Solution:** Regularly express appreciation for your husband's presence in your life.

3. Conflict or Misunderstanding

Disagreements can strain your friendship.

- **Solution:** Handle conflicts with care and focus on resolving them constructively.

Reflection Questions

- Do you see your husband as your friend as well as your spouse?

- What are some activities or hobbies you can enjoy together to deepen your friendship?

- How can you better support and encourage your husband as a friend?

Building a strong friendship with your husband is one of the most rewarding investments you can make in your marriage. When your relationship is grounded in friendship, you create a partnership that thrives on trust, joy, and mutual support.

Friendship isn't about grand gestures—it's about the little things you do daily to show that you enjoy and value each other's company. Keep nurturing the friendship that brought you together, and your marriage will continue to grow stronger with each passing day.

CHAPTER 10
GROW TOGETHER SPIRITUALLY WITH GOD

The Power of Spiritual Connection in Marriage

Spiritual growth is a journey that can deepen your bond with God and your spouse. As you grow closer to God individually, the strength of your relationship as a couple can be greatly enhanced. Spirituality in marriage goes beyond attending church together—it is about developing a shared faith, growing in your relationship with God, and supporting each other through the ups and downs of life from a spiritual perspective. This chapter explores how to foster spiritual growth as a couple and the profound impact it can have on your marriage.

Why Spiritual Growth is Crucial in Marriage

1. Strengthening Your Marriage with God's Presence

When you invite God into your marriage, He becomes the center that holds everything together. A strong spiritual foundation provides a sense of purpose, peace, and direction, even when faced with challenges.

- **Divine Guidance:** Prayer and faith offer wisdom and understanding when navigating difficult decisions or conflicts.

- **Shared Purpose:** Growing spiritually together helps align your values, goals, and desires with God's will for your relationship.

- **A Source of Strength:** When life is difficult, a shared faith in God gives you both the strength and hope to overcome challenges.

2. Nurturing Emotional Intimacy

Spiritual intimacy is deeply connected to emotional intimacy. Sharing your beliefs, praying together, and talking about your spiritual journey fosters an even deeper bond between you and your husband.

- **Vulnerability:** Spiritual conversations allow you to be vulnerable and open with one another in a safe, non-judgmental space.

- **Shared Values:** As you both align your hearts with God's values, you grow closer in your emotional connection and understanding of each other.

3. Encouraging Personal Growth

Spiritual growth isn't just about your marriage—it's about your individual journeys as well. As you both grow closer to God, you also grow in your character, kindness, patience, and love for each other.

- **Becoming Better Partners:** A stronger relationship with God leads to greater love, forgiveness, and empathy, which in turn enhances your relationship.

- **Accountability and Encouragement:** A spiritually connected marriage allows you to encourage each other to live according to biblical principles and hold each other accountable to your personal spiritual goals.

How to Grow Together Spiritually

1. Pray Together

Prayer is one of the most powerful ways to connect spiritually as a couple. It opens the door for God's presence in your marriage and invites His guidance into your daily lives.

- **Daily Prayer:** Set aside time to pray together each day, whether in the morning, before meals, or before bed. Pray for each other, your marriage, your family, and the challenges you face.

- **Pray in Moments of Struggle:** When difficulties arise, praying together can provide comfort and bring you closer.

- **Be Vulnerable in Prayer:** Don't be afraid to express your deepest hopes, fears, and desires to God and each other in your prayers.

2. Study the Bible Together

Spending time in God's Word helps you both grow spiritually and provides a source of wisdom and encouragement for your relationship.

- **Daily or Weekly Devotionals:** Set aside time each week or day to read scripture together, reflecting on its application in your marriage and life.

- **Discuss Scriptures:** After reading, talk about the verses you've read and how they apply to your marriage. Sharing your thoughts can help you grow in understanding and bring you closer.

- **Memorize Scripture Together:** Commit Bible verses to memory as a couple, particularly those that encourage love, patience, and kindness.

3. Attend Church Together

Attending church together strengthens your bond as a couple and provides an opportunity to worship and grow in faith alongside other believers.

- **Consistent Church Attendance:** Make it a priority to attend church services together, even if it means adjusting your schedule.

- **Get Involved:** Serve together in church ministries or volunteer opportunities. When you serve others as a couple, it deepens your connection to both God and each other.

4. Support Each Other's Individual Spiritual Growth

While growing spiritually together is essential, it's equally important to support each other in your individual relationships with God.

- **Encourage Personal Devotions:** Encourage your spouse to have their own quiet time with God, where they can grow in their faith independently.

- **Share Your Spiritual Journeys:** Share insights from your personal devotions and be open to discussing how God is working in your life.

- **Pray for Each Other's Personal Growth:** Lift up your spouse's spiritual journey in prayer, asking God to strengthen and guide them.

5. Serve God Together

Serving together as a couple creates opportunities to put your faith into action and strengthens your shared mission as a married couple.

- **Mission Work:** Volunteer together for missions, whether in your community or abroad, to spread God's love and compassion.

- **Serve Each Other:** Support each other in your personal or spiritual endeavors, whether it's helping with a project or providing emotional support during a challenging time.

- **Be a Witness Together:** Live out your faith publicly as a couple, showing love, kindness, and grace to others.

The Spiritual Impact on Your Marriage

1. Building Stronger Trust

As you both grow closer to God, you develop a deeper trust in each other. Knowing that God is at the center of your marriage brings peace and confidence that He will guide you through difficult moments.

- **Trust** in God's Timing: Even during moments of uncertainty or struggle, trusting that God is in control can strengthen your ability to trust each other.

2. Healing and Forgiveness

Spiritual growth brings healing and encourages forgiveness. The more you grow in your faith, the more you can practice God's grace and mercy with each other.

- **Forgiveness in Action:** By forgiving each other as Christ forgives, you create an environment of grace and healing in your marriage.

- **Healing Through Prayer:** Prayer can heal wounds caused by misunderstandings, hurts, or past mistakes. When you seek God's healing together, you restore your connection and move forward in love.

3. Living with Purpose and Direction

Growing together spiritually aligns your marriage with God's purpose, providing clarity on how to handle challenges, raise children, and build a future together.

- **Purposeful Decision-Making:** Let your faith guide major decisions in your marriage, from career choices to finances to family planning.

- **Shared Goals and Vision:** A shared spiritual vision helps you both work toward the same goals and provides a sense of unity in your journey together.

Challenges in Growing Spiritually Together

1. Time Constraints

It's easy to get caught up in the busyness of life and forget to prioritize spiritual growth together.

- **Solution:** Be intentional about setting aside time for prayer, Bible study, and attending church. Consider integrating these activities into your daily or weekly routines.

2. Differences in Spiritual Maturity

You may find that one partner is more spiritually mature than the other, which can create imbalance or frustration.

- **Solution:** Be patient and understanding, allowing each other to grow at your own pace. Support one another in your spiritual journeys and encourage growth without judgment.

3. Spiritual Discouragement

There may be seasons where one or both of you experience spiritual dryness or doubt.

- **Solution:** During these times, pray together for strength and trust that God is working in your lives. Encourage each other and remember that spiritual growth often involves ups and downs.

Reflection Questions

- How can you prioritize spiritual activities in your marriage?

- What is one way you and your spouse can support each other's spiritual growth?

- What role does God play in your marriage, and how can you invite Him into your relationship more intentionally?

Growing together spiritually with God is one of the most profound ways to strengthen your marriage. By praying together, studying scripture, serving together, and supporting each other's spiritual journeys, you build a bond that transcends earthly challenges. As you grow closer to God, you also grow closer to each other, becoming a united force that reflects God's love and grace in your marriage. Let your faith guide you and transform your relationship, and your marriage will flourish in ways beyond what you can imagine.

BONUS CHAPTER
HEALING THROUGH LOVE AND KINDNESS

Every marriage faces challenges, but when the relationship feels strained or distant, it can be difficult to see the way forward. In moments of struggle, the natural response may be frustration, criticism, or withdrawal. However, the Bible teaches us a different approach: one rooted in love, kindness, and grace. By choosing to respond with love and kindness, you invite God to work in your marriage, soften hearts, and bring restoration.

This chapter focuses on how to draw your husband closer, even when the marriage feels fragile, using biblical principles and practical steps to rebuild trust, connection, and unity.

The Power of Love and Kindness

Love and kindness are transformative forces in a marriage. They can break down walls of bitterness, foster emotional safety, and open the door for reconciliation.

1. Love Covers Over Faults

"Above all, love each other deeply, because love covers over a multitude of sins." (1 Peter 4:8)

Deep love has the power to overlook imperfections and extend grace. When your husband feels loved despite his flaws, it can soften his heart and open the door for healing.

2. Kindness Reflects God's Character

"Be kind and compassionate to one another, forgiving each other, just as in Christ God forgave you." (Ephesians 4:32)

Kindness is a reflection of God's love and mercy. When you treat your husband with kindness, even in challenging times, you mirror God's unconditional love.

3. Love and Kindness Break Barriers

"A gentle answer turns away wrath, but a harsh word stirs up anger." (Proverbs 15:1)

In moments of conflict, a gentle and loving response can de-escalate tension and create an atmosphere of peace.

Steps to Draw Your Husband Closer

When your marriage feels strained, the following steps can help you draw your husband back with love and kindness:

1. Commit to Prayer

Prayer is the foundation for healing in any marriage. Bring your struggles to God, asking Him to soften both your hearts, provide wisdom, and guide your actions.

"The Lord is near to all who call on him, to all who call on him in truth." (Psalm 145:18)

Pray for:

- God to work in your husband's heart.

- Patience and strength to love him unconditionally.

- Healing and restoration for your marriage.

2. Choose Love, Even When It's Hard

Love in marriage is not just an emotion; it's a choice. Show your husband love even when you don't feel like it. Acts of love, no matter how small, can reignite the connection between you.

"Let us not love with words or speech but with actions and in truth." (1 John 3:18)

Ways to show love:

- Cook his favorite meal.

- Leave a note expressing gratitude for him.

- Offer a kind gesture, like a hug or an encouraging word.

3. Speak Words of Encouragement

Harsh words can deepen divides, but affirming words can rebuild bridges. Use your words to encourage, uplift, and reassure your husband of your commitment.

"Do not let any unwholesome talk come out of your mouths, but only what is helpful for building others up according to their needs." (Ephesians 4:29)

Examples of affirmations:

- "I believe in you, and I'm here to support you."

- "I know we're going through a tough time, but I'm committed to working through this together."

- "I love you and value all you do for our family."

4. Create a Safe Space

A strained marriage often results in emotional walls. Show your husband that your relationship is a safe space where he can share his thoughts and feelings without fear of judgment or criticism.

"Do to others as you would have them do to you." (Luke 6:31)

To create safety:

- Listen without interrupting.

- Avoid blaming or accusing language.

- Be patient as he opens up.

5. Focus on Positive Actions

Small, consistent acts of kindness can have a big impact on your marriage. By choosing to serve your husband with love, you set the tone for reconciliation.

"Let all that you do be done in love." (1 Corinthians 16:14)

Acts of kindness:

- Offer to help him with a task he's been struggling with.

- Surprise him with something thoughtful, like a handwritten letter or his favorite snack.

- Give him space to relax and unwind when he's feeling overwhelmed.

6. Trust God with the Outcome

Ultimately, the healing of your marriage is in God's hands. While you can take steps to show love and kindness, it's God who works in both of your hearts to bring restoration. Surrender your marriage to Him, trusting in His timing and plan.

"Trust in the Lord with all your heart and lean not on your own understanding; in all your ways submit to him, and he will make your paths straight." (Proverbs 3:5-6)

When Love and Kindness Feel One-Sided

In some situations, showing love and kindness may feel like a one-sided effort. Remember that your actions are not just for your husband but also for God. Your faithfulness to God's call to love and serve your spouse is an act of worship and obedience.

"And let us not grow weary of doing good, for in due season we will reap, if we do not give up." (Galatians 6:9)

Reflection Questions

- How can you show love and kindness to your husband today, even in the midst of challenges?

- Are there areas in your marriage where you need to respond with gentleness instead of frustration?

- How can prayer help you find strength and guidance during this season?

Drawing your husband closer with love and kindness, even when your marriage feels rocky, is a reflection of God's transformative love. By choosing to respond with grace, patience, and gentleness, you create a path for healing and restoration. Trust in God's ability to mend what feels broken and remain faithful to the call to love your husband unconditionally. As you walk this journey, may your actions glorify God and serve as a testament to His power to redeem and restore.

CONCLUSION
GROWING IN LOVE DAILY

As you come to the end of this journey through, *We Still Do*, it's important to recognize that loving your spouse is not a one-time effort but a lifelong commitment. The principles explored in this book—communication, appreciation, quality time, support, affection, conflict resolution, shared responsibilities, humor, friendship, spiritual growth, and partnership—are not just individual actions, but habits that, when consistently nurtured, create the foundation for a deep, lasting marriage.

Marriage, like any relationship, is dynamic. It evolves over time, facing challenges, changes, and transitions. However, when the principles of love are actively practiced and strengthened, your relationship will not only endure but thrive. As you continue to grow together, remember that love is more than a feeling—it is a choice, a decision made each day to prioritize your husband, to invest in the relationship, and to actively choose grace, patience, and kindness.

Reflections on the Journey

Throughout the pages of this book, you've explored how to communicate openly, show appreciation, prioritize quality time, support his dreams, and be affectionate. You've learned the importance of handling conflict with care, sharing responsibilities, maintaining humor, building a strong friendship, and growing spiritually together. Each of these elements plays a vital role in creating a healthy, thriving marriage. The key to unlocking these actions is consistency and intention.

It's important to recognize that loving your husband doesn't mean being perfect. No marriage is without challenges, and there will be moments where things don't go as planned. However, when you approach your marriage with a heart that seeks to understand, uplift, and honor your spouse, the strength of your love will endure even in difficult times. Every small act of love—whether it's a kind word, a shared prayer, or a quiet moment of togetherness—adds up over time to create a bond that is unbreakable.

Embrace the Adventure of Marriage

Marriage is not static; it's a living, breathing partnership that requires ongoing attention and care. As you grow individually and as a couple, embrace the opportunity to continually learn about each other, grow spiritually together, and support one another's dreams. This journey is an adventure, and when you walk through it side by side with a heart full of love, respect, and commitment, the possibilities are endless.

Remember, the most beautiful marriages aren't those without conflict or difficulty, but those where both partners choose to remain committed to love, to each other, and to the growth of their relationship. It is through this process of growing and learning together that your marriage becomes a reflection of God's love—a love that is unconditional, sacrificial, and eternal.

Loving your husband is a journey that never ends. Each day presents new opportunities to deepen your connection, to understand one another more fully, and to grow closer to God as individuals and as partners. This book offers a blueprint, but the real work of love is done in the moments you choose to prioritize your marriage and invest in the person you've committed your life to.

May you always seek to love your husband with purpose, grace, and devotion. As you walk this path together, may your marriage be a testament to the power of love, faith, and commitment. Let your relationship reflect the beauty of a partnership where both people grow, laugh, and love in the presence of God, knowing that the best chapters of your marriage are still to come.

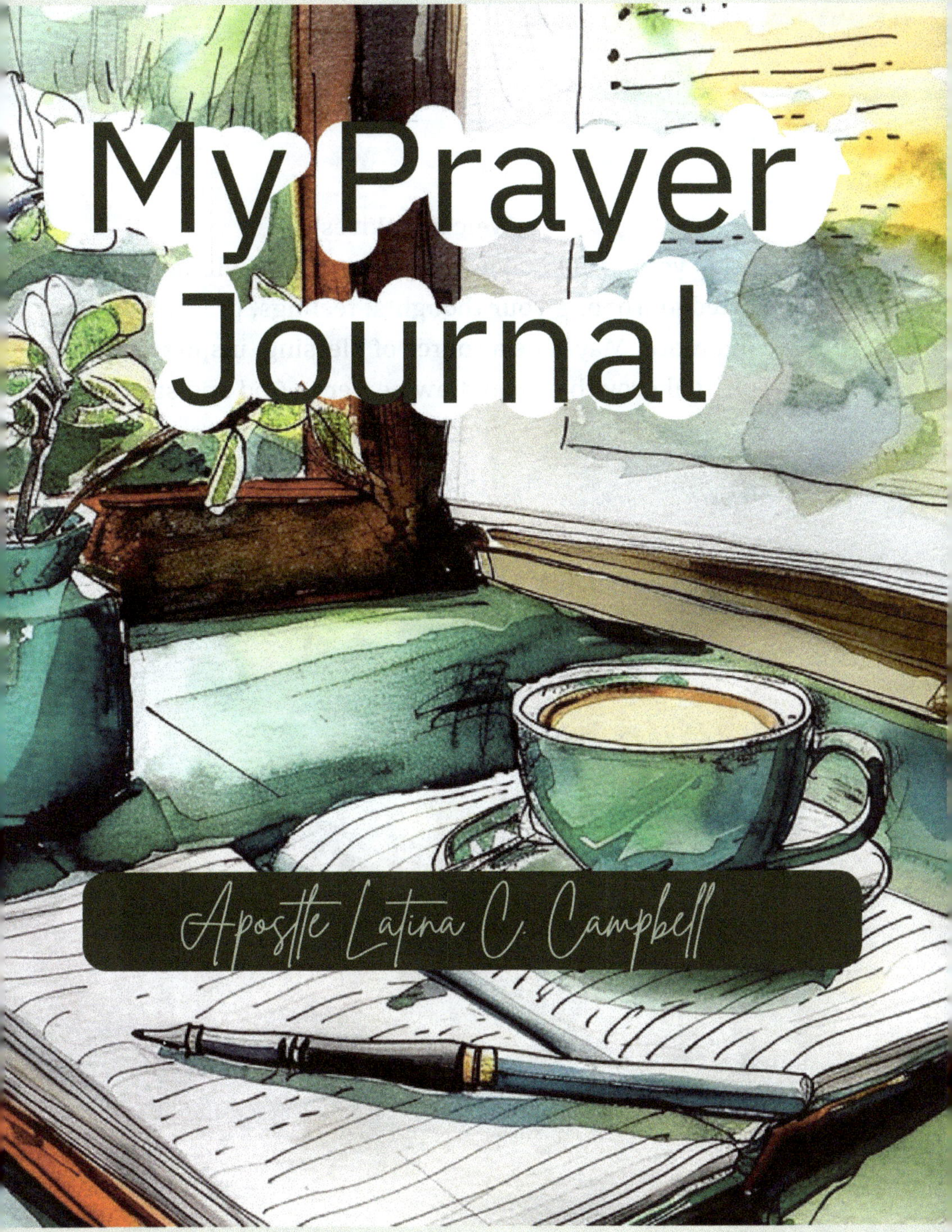
My Prayer Journal
Apostle Latina C. Campbell

Welcome Wives!
Inside you'll find 40 journal prompts that will help you get started journaling your thoughts, feelings, prayers, praises, and more! May it be a source of blessing, inspiration, and spiritual growth as you draw nearer to God and strengthen your marriage.

-Apostle Latina C. Campbell

Reflect on your day and write down three things you're thankful for.

Write a letter to God expressing your thoughts, feelings, and hopes for the future.

Describe a challenge you're facing and ask God for guidance and strength in overcoming it.

List three people in your life and pray for their well-being and any specific needs they may have.

Write down a Bible verse that speaks to you and journal about its significance in your life.

Reflect on a recent answered prayer and thank God for His faithfulness.

Journal about a struggle or fear you're experiencing and surrender it to God in prayer.

_____
_____
_____
_____
_____
_____
_____
_____
_____
_____
_____
_____
_____
_____
_____
_____
_____
_____
_____
_____
_____
_____

Write down a question you have for God and spend some time listening for His response.

*Describe a moment of joy or blessing you experienced
today and thank God for it.*

Make a list of things you're worried about and give each one over to God in prayer.

Reflect on a mistake you made and ask God for forgiveness and guidance in learning from it.

Write down a characteristic of God that you admire and reflect on how you can emulate it in your own life.

Describe a person who inspires you and pray for God's blessing and guidance in their life.

List three things you're struggling with and ask God for His peace and presence in the midst of them.

Write down a goal or dream you have and ask God for His wisdom and direction in pursuing it. OR ask God if you should pursue it or not.

Reflect on a recent encounter with someone and pray for God's love to be evident in your interactions with them.

Describe a moment when you felt God's presence today and thank Him for it.

Write a prayer of surrender, offering all your worries, fears, and hopes to God

List three things you're looking forward to and thank God for the blessings He has in store for you.

Reflect on a passage of Scripture you read today and journal about how it applies to your life.

Reflect on Psalm 23:1-3 and write about how God has been your shepherd, providing guidance and comfort in your life.

Meditate on Philippians 4:6-7 and journal about surrendering your worries to God and experiencing His peace.

Consider Matthew 6:33 and contemplate how you can seek God's kingdom first in your daily life through prayer and action.

Reflect on Romans 12:2 and write about how God can transform your mind and renew your perspective through prayer.

Meditate on James 1:5-6 and journal about asking God for wisdom in difficult situations and trusting Him to provide.

_____

_____

_____

_____

_____

_____

_____

_____

_____

_____

_____

_____

_____

_____

_____

_____

_____

_____

_____

_____

_____

_____

Consider Psalm 46:10 and reflect on the importance of being still in God's presence during prayer.

Reflect on Isaiah 40:31 and write about finding strength and renewal in God through prayer during times of weariness.

Meditate on 1 Thessalonians 5:16–18 and journal about cultivating a spirit of gratitude through prayer in all circumstances.

Consider Matthew 26:41 and reflect on the importance of prayer in overcoming temptation and staying spiritually alert.

Reflect on Philippians 2:3-4 and write about praying for humility and a servant's heart in your interactions with others.

Meditate on Colossians 4:2 and journal about the significance of being persistent and devoted in prayer.

Consider Psalm 51:10 and reflect on praying for God to create a clean heart and renew a steadfast spirit within you.

Read Hebrews 11:1 and describe a moment when you had to rely on faith rather than sight in your walk with God.

*Meditate on Ephesians 3:20-21 and journal about
praying for God's power to work within you and to do
immeasurably more than you can ask or imagine.*

Consider Romans 8:26-27 and reflect on the Holy Spirit's role in interceding for you in prayer when you don't know what to pray for.

Reflect on Proverbs 3:5–6 and write about trusting in the Lord with all your heart and seeking His guidance through prayer.

Meditate on Matthew 7:7-8 and journal about persistently asking, seeking, and knocking in prayer, trusting that God will answer.

Consider 1 John 1:9 and reflect on confessing your sins to God in prayer and experiencing His forgiveness and cleansing.

Reflect on Hebrews 4:16 and write about boldly approaching God's throne of grace in prayer to receive mercy and find grace in times of need.

Meditate on Luke 18:1–8 and journal about persevering in prayer like the persistent widow, trusting that God will bring justice in His perfect timing.

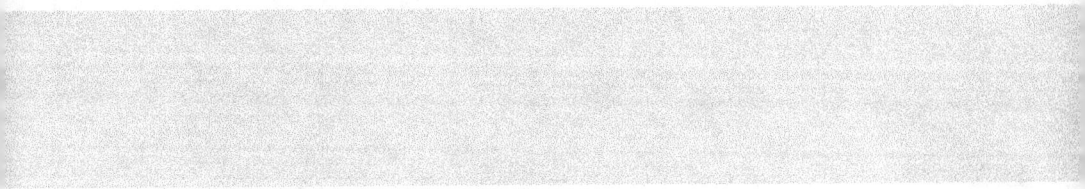

www.ingramcontent.com/pod-product-compliance
Lightning Source LLC
Chambersburg PA
CBHW060244030426
42335CB00014B/1588